Unwavering

Faith

CONFIDENT

PATIENCE

CHARLES RICHARDSON

Unwavering Faith

CONFIDENT PATIENCE

DAkpabli

DAKPABLI & ASSOCIATES
ACCRA

ISBN for this Edition: 97899889023 7 7

Editor: Efua Richardson Dimado, EditConsult Inc.

Book Layout by multiPIXEL Limited
P.O. Box DC 1965, Dansoman, Accra, Ghana
Email: jkojoyanney@gmail.com
Tel: +233 302 333 502 | +233 246 725 060 | +233 246 210 862

Published by
DAkpabli & Associates
P O Box 7465, Accra North, Accra, Ghana
Tel: +233 264 339 066 | +233 244 704 250 | +233 247 896 375
Email: info@dakpabli.com

This book is dedicated to my wife Patricia who stood by me, prayed for me and took courageous steps of faith with me as the greatest trial of my life unfolded.

She has proven to be a true Proverbs 31 woman since we embarked on our journey together. I cherish her love and companionship as we continue to navigate under God's guidance to our glorious destinies.

ACKNOWLEDGEMENTS

My profound gratitude goes to my Lord Jesus Christ. I thank Him for the opportunity to prove that, indeed, His Word is true and that I can lean all of my weight on His promises.

I also wish to thank those who were there for me in diverse ways as the story unfolded in real time. I want to especially make mention of:

my spiritual fathers
Bishop Dag Heward-Mills, Prophet Kakra Baiden, both of the United Denominations Originating from the Lighthouse Group of Churches (UDOLGC), and Pastor Enoch Adeboye, Redeemed Christian Church of God (RCCG).

my spiritual family in Abu Dhabi
Matt and Rana Jones, Anne Jennings-Plenkovich, Brendan and Linda Law, Ranvir and Susan Toor, Grant Jeffery, John and Sylee Savio, Sydney and Tsitsi Husayiwhevu, Winnie Lengalenga, and our friends at Cornerstone Church and Evangelical Community Church (ECC).

I equally wish to thank Kurankyi and Eliz Dadson, Ernest and Asantewa Engmann, Charles Ahene, Francis and Celia Danboyi, Kofi and Nardu Agyeman Pastor Zeal – RCCG, His Excellency Sheikh Shakboot.

the medical team

Dr. Muhammed Shaffiq, Nurse Alice and the medical team that took care of me at the Sheikh Khalifa Medical City(SKMC), Abu Dhabi, UAE.

my family

My dad Ebenezer Richardson, my siblings Sam, Nancy, Evelyn, James and Vivian. Special thanks to SM and Sally Quartey, my big-hearted sister in-law, Wendy Mensah, and my aunt Grace Richardson among many others.

This section of the book would easily become a volume by itself if I continued any further. To those of you who are not mentioned here specifically, I wish to express my profuse thanks for your support. May God bless you abundantly!

Finally, I wish to thank my brother-in-law Nana Awere Damoah and his publishing team, as well as my sister Evelyn Dimado for their invaluable assistance in converting the story from a manuscript into a real book which I believe will be a blessing to many. May God bless you immensely!

CONTENTS

FOREWORD

The writer to the book of Hebrews admonishes us in verse 12 of the sixth chapter to imitate those who through faith and patience inherit the promises. "…that you do not become sluggish but imitate those who through faith and patience inherit the promises." – Hebrews 6:12, NKJV

There are indeed a lot of promises that God has made to us His children in His Word, all of which are yes, and amen, in Christ Jesus. "For all the promises of God in Him are Yes, and in Him Amen, to the glory of God through us." – 2 Corinthians 1: 20, NKJV

From a ringside position, as it were, I have had the privilege of witnessing what God's faithfulness and man's inexorable faith can do, as far as just one of those promises is concerned – healing. God promised that if we serve Him He will take sickness away from our midst (Exodus 33:25). I was privy to the unfolding of this stupendous story of how God turned around a literal 'grave' situation into a medically confounding miracle of healing.

As a believer, a medical doctor, and Charles' spouse, my whole perspective on sickness and disease underwent a paradigm shift during this period. I saw unwavering faith and confident patience dovetail seamlessly to release the power of God that resulted in this awesome miracle. I am grateful to God for this testimony to His faithfulness and I am inspired by the tenacious faith of Charles throughout this episode.

Indeed, this book was written in compliance with an instruction from the flabbergasted Muslim lead physician when Charles was discharged from hospital. Driven by the conviction that it was actually God who wanted him to document this testimony, he has finally produced this account and I am truly honoured and grateful for the privilege of penning the Foreword.

I thank God for this awesome miracle and acknowledge Charles for his obedience to the instruction to write a book. I am certain that after following the story to its very end, the reader will experience the same paradigm shift in their perspective on sickness and disease as I did. It is my prayer, above all, that many will be strengthened in their faith, more awesome testimonies will emerge and countless souls will be converted to God and established in His Kingdom. To God alone be the glory!

Patricia Richardson
Accra, Ghana
July 03, 2020

PROLOGUE

In April 2009, I had the opportunity of taking up a permanent position in a company in Abu Dhabi that I had previously been involved with on contract basis. One of the reasons I was drawn to this offer was the prospect of a more regular shift pattern than what I had experienced thus far in my career.

Working shifts was a part and parcel of my working life as a licensed aircraft engineer so being together with my family was something I did not take for granted. Invariably my personal plans had to be structured around my work roster, and for a season I did not even get to enjoy two consecutive days off! So this opportunity really afforded me the luxury, as it were, of being together with my family most of the time, and also having a more regular and predictable work schedule.

So I did take up the offer and the following year the rest of the family relocated to join me in Abu Dhabi, in the United Arab Emirates. Trish rightly observed that probably for the first time since we got married, we were spending a lot more time together.

In March 2012 I lost my job and didn't feel led to immediately leave the country as a lot of people do, probably due to the fact that most residence permits granted to expatriates are work-based. I took up a couple of private tuition contracts in the meantime while I searched for new opportunities within the country, but all the available local leads eventually proved futile.

A year and a half later, I was invited to an interview by a company in Qatar and was successful. Glory be to God! I was very excited and shared this testimony in church. The company graciously granted me the option of determining a start date which I fixed within the next school vacation, after the second term, in order that we would all return to Ghana and then I would proceed to Qatar after a couple of weeks.

But during this time of waiting, the biggest storm since I arrived on the earth hit me almost out of the blue....*Wham!* I was caught right in its eye and suddenly everything I was doing or thinking about receded into an abyss of insignificance as I tried to come to terms with what was unfolding in my body. This was a very rude awakening and I could feel my life literally ebbing away. Through it all, however, my Father and my God had my back, and He brought me out unscathed! All praise and thanks be to Him!

May you be blessed and may your faith in Him be strengthened as you walk beside me through this most somber chapter of my life and see how awesome and faithful God is! A God who keeps covenant with His people and has the final say in their affairs!!

WHAT'S GOING ON?

On the beautiful morning of March 1, 2014, just as the orange glow of the rising sun began to assert itself progressively over the horizon, I decided to don my jogging gear and do a couple of laps around the block. I have always believed in bodily exercise being of some benefit (1 Timothy 4:8) and consciously indulged in cardiovascular and physical workouts to keep this temple of God in good shape.

Barely a couple of minutes into this, more or less, regular routine I detected something rather abnormal about my breathing. I noticed that I was running out of breath and energy much sooner than usual. I wondered what could be happening and decided to abandon my early morning fitness regime and beat a slow retreat home.

Once the front door was shut behind me, I made a beeline for the kitchen to fix myself a warm sweet drink to pep my energy levels up. In between sips of my favourite 'Ovaltine' chocolate beverage I contemplated this rather foreboding development, which had totally messed up my morning plans, and what mishap it might portend.

I had been coughing for a couple of weeks, but these were dry, sporadic bouts of coughing to which I had hardly paid any attention. These coughs invariably just went away the same way they came without much medical intervention. However, this one, I noticed, had lingered for much longer so after conferring with my wife, Trish, we went to see a doctor who diagnosed bronchitis and gave medication to clear it. After completing the course of treatment, the cough was still present, ridiculing me in the face every now and then. This development was rather unnerving and got me thinking a bit deeper.

I reminisced on how I had previously been healed a few months earlier of a brief spell of back pain that had racked my body for some weeks. In its latter stages I had to meticulously adhere to a particular sequence when getting out of bed, failing which a muscle spasm would just knock me down flat on my back. I couldn't reach to my toes when I bent over as I used to, and a simple activity like tying my shoelaces had become a tormenting ordeal. I was becoming dependent on pain-relief medication and I didn't want to go down that road.

Then one Thursday night, just before I clambered into bed, I realised I was down to the last dose of my medicine, whose soothing effect would surely wear off before dawn. I said a simple prayer thanking God that Jesus paid the price for my healing with the stripes He received on His back and as I took the last pill, clinging to His word, I believed that this would indeed be the last. Huge step of faith that was...but I had such a conviction about the truth of God's Word that I took the plunge.

I woke up normally the next morning and did not experience any pain at all! I got to church a bit early to help with the setting up of the hall for the service in the morning. I had to carry and rig up some equipment, with the help of my duty team members, and still did not experience a hint of pain! I carried out all my normal activities throughout the day without let or hindrance. 'Wow! Praise God!' I muttered to myself. I shared this testimony first with Trish and then with the church at the next meeting.

Equipped with such a powerful personal experience of God's healing power and standing on His word regarding the healing and divine health available to me as His redeemed son, I settled the matter in my heart that sickness was an oppression of the enemy and it had no right to remain in my body. Jesus' body was broken so that mine would be made whole (Isaiah 53:5). Jesus took my infirmities and carried away my sicknesses (Matthew 8:17), by whose stripes I was healed (1 Peter 2:24). I meditated on these scriptures and asserted them over my situation yet, there was no improvement in the cough.

It was remarkable that this development was coming in the wake of a breakthrough in my work situation. Having been out of work for a year-and-a-half, I had been offered a position in a company in Qatar and had shared this testimony of God's goodness with my church family. We were at this point waiting for our two boys to finish the second term at school so that we could leave Abu Dhabi and head towards Ghana, initially. I held fast to my confession but we decided to consult an internal medicine specialist first and so booked an appointment.

THE BOMBSHELL

On the day of the appointment we walked into the doctor's office and I reported the spell of persistent coughing, the shortness of breath as well as decreasing energy levels. After his initial examination he said that he couldn't detect anything unusual in my chest. However, he noticed that my pulse was very high and requested some tests to be done as well as an X-ray to be taken.

When we returned to the see this doctor the next day with the test results, he informed us that the indicators all read normal. He was at a complete loss though as to what could be responsible for the high pulse since my thyroid function, which he initially had concerns about, turned out to be normal. He then held up the X-ray film against a light source to scrutinise the image and his reaction was as startling as it was frightening.

First, he squinted as he peered closely at the image and then threw his head back as he held it higher up. The look on his face was one of palpable shock and incredulity as the histrionics continued for a while. We sat in front of the desk quite disturbed by all these ominous gestures, wondering what he was going to blurt out eventually. At this point, he broke the deafening silence by remarking that he could see extensive damage to my lungs, which probably began much earlier than when the first external symptoms of coughing appeared. He paused for a while and then dropped the bombshell, 'you have end-stage tuberculosis'.

Bam! Just like that. He explained that there were four stages in the evolution of the disease and so this was the terminal stage.

We were numbed, speechless for a while, as we pensively processed the doctor's grim diagnosis. I was in denial and only stopped short of blurting out loud, *I reject tuberculosis in the name of Jesus!*

What a shock! *Was I day-dreaming, or was this real?* I wondered. He indicated that I would have to choose between the option of going to a government hospital to receive further medical attention or heading back to my home country. He however suggested that we go and think about it for a day or so. *Phew!*

A nurse brought a nose mask for me to don on, followed by a group of curious medical staff who had piled themselves up at the door, jostling to catch a glimpse of me. Obviously, word had begun to spread in the facility about my case, and I could feel the weight of their gazes as they peered at me with concern. We left the doctor's office, went outside to the car, where we sat for about five minutes without exchanging a single word, as we gauged the weightiness of all that had transpired in the doctor's office. This was shattering!

I finally started the car engine, backed out of the parking lot, and hit the road in the direction of our home. Only then did we both find some energy to reject any sickness and infirmity that was trying to fasten itself on me in the name of Jesus.

"If any two of you agree on earth as to asking anything in my Name, it shall be done for them by my Father who is in heaven" – Matthew 18:19

Trish and I resolved to stand on the Word of God no matter what, as we hit the road for the fifty-odd kilometre journey home. Truly, it had been an eventful day indeed.

That night, after our two boys, Jude and Josh had retired, we spread all the medical documents on the floor before the Lord. I recalled the response of king Hezekiah in the scriptures when he received a threatening letter delivered by messengers from the king of Assyria.

"And Hezekiah received the letter from the hand of the messengers and read it. And Hezekiah went up to the house of the Lord and spread it before the Lord." – 2 Kings 19:14

This was the moment when truth would have to prevail over fact. We took authority over this attack by the enemy and deployed the shield of faith, confessing that Jesus took our infirmities and carried away our sicknesses (Matthew 8:17) and I claimed that by His stripes I was already healed (1 Pet. 2:24). No sickness could remain in my body because it is the temple of the Holy Spirit. We just poured out our hearts to the Lord and confessed the truth of God's Word over the situation. Then, we went to bed.

I woke up the next day and didn't feel any better at all. On the contrary, the shortness of breath was getting worse and I was also feeling weaker after 'normal' routine activity. I remained steadfast in my declaration that by His stripes I was healed and I believed and understood that it was a finished work yet the physical symptoms lingered. We decided to go and see an internist at one of the major hospitals in the city. He listened to my chest and remarked that he was unable to pick up anything unusual. While I lay on the examining bed, he went to his desk and after scrutinising the X-ray image that Trish showed him I overheard him say, "your husband has tuberculosis". He asked me to dress up while Trish challenged his diagnosis, pointing out that there were other conditions which could produce that X-ray image.

After excusing himself to consult the radiologist for well over thirty minutes, he re-appeared to concede that although her argument was plausible most doctors in that jurisdiction would come to the same conclusion.

We made one final appointment to see a lung specialist this time, who after conducting his physical and laboratory examinations, informed us that he suspected strongly that it was a case of tuberculosis and proceeded to refer me to the premier public hospital. At this stage, I was really drained of energy and was experiencing severe shortness of breath when I walked for a few metres. How inundating!

This was happening in the wake of sharing testimonies in church of God's faithfulness in how I received healing from acute back pain and how I had been offered a desired job in a company in Qatar. Everything was just swirling in my mind now as I tried to process all these developments, but I still believed that God is good. We returned home quite exhausted, emotionally and physically. Trish and I spent some time in prayer and continued to confess scriptures on healing. I decided I'd have to check into the hospital the next day.

IN THE LION'S DEN

The morning of March 19, 2014 is one that will forever be etched on my memory. I checked into the hospital after doing the school run and tucked into what little breakfast my diminishing appetite could tolerate. After walking a short distance from the car park to the emergency isolation department of the hospital where I'd been referred to, I was palpably labouring in my breathing so I was met with a wheelchair in which I was transported into the hospital. After checking the details of my referral from their data system, I was informed that I would be admitted anyway although my health insurance card was not accepted in that hospital. A nose mask was placed over my face and I was taken to a room in the intensive care unit of the department.

I was made to understand that I had been quarantined and that only the medical staff and my spouse had access to my room. Within moments my vitals were taken, I was helped to change into a hospital gown and an adult diaper. I was laid on a bed that had a cluster of monitoring equipment at the headboard. Some sensors were attached to my chest while an oxygen mask was placed over my face. As I looked round at the array of equipment and the grim pairs of eyes fixed on me, I realised that I was literally in the lion's den, with the icy claws of this dreadful disease dangling ominously close. The admitting doctor informed me that it was a very bad case and his facial expression was even more foreboding. I was very knackered at this point and my mind was just swirling, trying to process what was unfolding before my very eyes. I drifted into sleep on this wave of mental activity.

The next morning, Trish actually got a call from the hospital while on her way to see me. The doctor wanted to see her urgently. Once she arrived, without the courtesy of even ensuring privacy, the doctor asked her if she was ready for what was going to happen.

"How many children do you have?", he blurted. "Are you ready for what is about to happen?", he continued.

"Like what?", she asked.

"You are a doctor so you should know." (He had come to know her profession during an earlier interaction with her).

"I think you should inform your embassy to get ready to transport a dead body back to your country."

Now, what professional arrogance!! This doctor had definitely overstepped his bounds by trying to play God this time around. I knew the enemy was behind this attack on my health and I had to decide whose report to believe – God's or the doctor's. Trish and I decided to agree and still stand on the eternal truth of God's word.

The next day I felt more ill and noticed that I was losing weight so rapidly it had begun to show visibly. I had been put on oxygen continuously, and the mask was only removed momentarily to enable me to eat a few morsels of food, by which time the alerts on the monitors would be sounding. My oxygen saturation, which was normally supposed to be 95-plus per cent had plummeted to 87 per cent. I was informed that my left lung had collapsed and the other one had developed a hole that was leaking air into my chest cavity. I had developed what the medics call a pneumothorax in my right lung. In short, my chest was 'a mess', per the doctor.

Trish was invited into the lead doctor's consulting room to view the x-ray images for herself, as they had come to know that she is a doctor. However, she declined to look at any 'medical evidence' of what was assailing me, and only wanted to know what their intended course of action was. They indicated that they would put me on strong antibiotics to deal with a chest infection and then put me on a course of TB treatment to fight the bacteria. However, from the team leader's body language and pronouncements it was evident they had all but given up on me.

After six weeks of being confined to bed, a physiotherapist was brought in to help me do some exercises, as the doctor was concerned about muscle weakness and bed sores. All I could do during the first session was to stand, with a lot of assistance, and then sit again on my bed. I was almost breathless after this thirty-second activity. I was quite shocked: my leg muscles were completely gone! I had to learn to take baby steps all over again, like a toddler. Fortunately, the physiotherapist was a Christian lady and she encouraged me a great deal during the sessions. At this stage, my body weight had plummeted to fifty–three kilograms from a sturdy seventy-eight! I was just a bag of skin and bones!!

The dramatic downward spiral of wasting away continued unabated and it had become a real struggle to breathe without oxygen. I held fast to my faith and continued to relentlessly declare the truth of God's Word and claim it as I trusted Him for complete healing:

> *"I shall not die but live, and declare the works of the Lord."* – Psalms 118:17

> *"...by whose stripes you were healed"* – 1 Peter 2:24

"…that it might be fulfilled which was spoken by the prophet Isaiah saying: He Himself took our infirmities and bore our sicknesses" – Matthew 8:17

'For I will restore health to you and heal you of your wounds, says the Lord…" –Jeremiah 30:17

"But He was wounded for our transgressions, he was bruised for our iniquities; the chastisement for our peace was upon Him, and by His stripes we are healed." – Isaiah 53:5

I stood in agreement with Trish and kept on affirming these scriptures in the face of contrary evidence. I was very careful not to let any word proceed from my lips that would contradict the Word of God.

Whenever the doctors came to check on me and asked me how I was feeling, I always told them I was fine. I had no idea that the lead doctor found this very irritating until on one occasion he turned around to ask me, "why do you keep saying you are fine when I ask you how you are feeling?"

My answer to him was, "because that is what I believe and that is how I feel."

He looked quite perplexed because he, obviously, could not pick up any signals of worry or fear from me following the grim prognosis that he had slapped on me. For me this was truly a fight of faith and the challenge was to never lose focus of the truth of His word.

One evening the duty doctor informed me that they had to perform an emergency procedure. They explained that they had to insert a chest tube to drain air that was leaking into my chest cavity in order to improve my breathing. Trish had already left for home so I had them call her to give her the details and to ask her if I should go ahead to sign the consent form for them to go ahead. She said it was okay to sign the consent form, so I did.

The surgeon explained to me that I would be put under local anaesthesia and that there would be a little pain at a point. However, it turned out to be the most painful procedure I have ever undergone in my entire life! Little wonder, I never set eyes on that particular surgeon again until I left the hospital. Now in addition to the sensors elsewhere on my chest, there was this half-inch tube poking out of my chest and connected to a suction pump.

The way the interns peered at the equipment and then at me whenever they followed the lead doctor into my room made me realise that my case had evolved into one of significant academic interest. Surely, I was not supposed to be a specimen for the curiosity of medical student? I vividly recall that we had responded to invitations from a nurse friend of ours to pray for her patients on a couple of occasions at this very hospital. Quite a paradox it was then to accept the reality that I was now a patient in a grave condition on admission at the same hospital.

There was some improvement in my breathing, but I was still hooked on to medical oxygen. My doctor informed me that I would need to undergo surgery on my lungs, and that arrangements were being made to have me transferred to another hospital which had a cardiothoracic specialist. Bam!! The thought of surgery on these delicate organs was scary. I muttered a prayer to My Father asking Him to perform the surgery Himself. Indeed, the healing was already mine and that was what I kept on declaring.

All this while, the church family at Cornerstone, where we fellowshipped, was praying for me; both the house group of which we were a part, as well as the larger congregation. One of our senior pastors in Lighthouse Chapel International, Prophet Kakra Baiden, also prayed with me over the phone when we called him and requested for prayer. Since I was in isolation, no visitor was allowed to my room except Trish.

One night, I was pleasantly surprised, when in my sleepy state I suddenly made out the familiar form of one of our friends in church, Grant, right by my bedside. For a moment I thought it was an angelic visitation. He had managed to break through the security to come over and see me, pray with me and even leave behind a birthday present for Jude, our son, who had turned twelve a few weeks earlier. Wow!

I had tremendous support from our close brothers and sisters of like precious faith. There was even a Christian nurse on the medical team, who took the great risk of praying with us whenever she found the opportunity. In this strong islamic territory, if any of her nosey colleagues found her out, they definitely wouldn't hesitate at all to report.

Some of our friends sent me a pile of books by Christian authors to read, which I did with relish, given all the time I had at my disposal. I had my laptop with me and had internet access so, except when I was asleep, I was always reading, watching or listening to Word-based inspirational stuff.

Some members of the medical team took notice of this; the lead doctor once asked me to share the gist of a book I was reading – *Destined to Reign*, by Joseph Prince – which I happily did. He just nodded and left the room with a wry smile on his face. On another occasion, the lady who took my meal choices told me she had overheard some Christian music coming from my laptop. Upon learning that I had been in quarantine for close to four months at that point, she confessed that she needed to repent of complaining to God about her situation of not finding herself in the job for which she had been originally trained.

Was I going to be hobbling around clutching onto an oxygen supply in one hand and a suction pump in the other? *Definitely not*! This was the deafening yet silent answer that reverberated through my inner being.

I did not accept at all for one moment, that this was my lot as a redeemed child of God. These were tough moments, as all I had to hang on to was the infallible Word of God. The more I spoke the Word over my situation, the more stubbornly the physical symptoms seemed to compete for my attention. In all of this, I was careful not to let any word come out from my mouth that was not in keeping with the scriptures I had affirmed and claimed concerning my healing. Trish and I simply agreed to maintain declaring scriptures over the situation even though the physical evidence was contrary.

> *"Again I say to you that if two of you agree on earth concerning anything that they ask, it will be done for them by my Father in heaven."* – Matthew 18:19

I had also been informed that there were bullae or air pockets in my lungs that would require surgery to remove. However, there was no cardiothoracic specialist in that hospital, and they were unable to secure a bed elsewhere. Eventually, when a bed became available, the cardiothoracic surgeon stipulated that he would only accept me if I tested negative for TB bacteria. I didn't even want to contemplate the prospect of surgery on my lungs! These were very delicate organs, not to even think of 'playing' around with them! I prayed and asked God to take over and perform the surgery Himself.

Not long after that, the chest tube fell out of my chest by itself after a brief bout of coughing. This is a tube that was supposed to have been sutured to my skin. I called the duty nurse and told her what had happened, but she obviously didn't believe my story and rather insinuated that I had yanked it out. I found out later that she had gone to write that in her notes. Within minutes, a team of doctors barged into my room looking visibly concerned. They inquired if I was experiencing any respiratory distress, to which I replied in the negative. They decided to leave the tube out in that case and cover up the entry hole.

I didn't have a doubt that God had 'kicked out' that tube in order to perform whatever surgery was needed Himself. Definitely an answer to prayer, albeit in a totally unexpected manner. Truly, there is no formula with God! His ways are indeed past finding out. The doctor returned again and again to inquire if my breathing was normal. I honestly didn't detect any change in my respiratory condition after the tube came out. This was a really amazing event beyond rational explanation in medical procedure. The doctors were visibly baffled but also relieved that I was not in any form of distress. God was definitely at work!

MAY TWENTY-SECOND

May 22, 2014 was a red-lettered day during my sojourn at the hospital. I was now out of intensive care but still in an isolation room. Early one morning, I was informed that I would be taken to the radiology department for an x-ray later in the day. That same morning, at home, Trish had a kind of open vision in which she saw herself being greeted by the nurse on duty as she arrived at the ward on her daily visit. In this vision, the nurse told her that I had just returned from the radiology department and that the x-ray results were good.

When she arrived at the hospital, as she approached the nurses' station leading to my room, behold, there was the same nurse she had seen in the vision speaking the exact same words to her! *Amazing!* This sounded really surreal as Trish recounted it to me when she entered my room. *Wow!* I could sense a shift in the atmosphere already. Exactly what it was, I couldn't really put a finger on yet.

It turned out that, later that afternoon, the medical team showed up in my room, led by the lead doctor with an unusually broad smile skimming across his countenance. Clearly, they were very happy with the latest set of images of my chest as they proceeded to announce the exciting development. The lung which had collapsed was now completely restored to its original form, and the hole could no more be seen in the other one. *Wow!* And this was without their intervention!!

They asked for my oxygen saturation to be checked and to their surprise that had also reverted to the normal level of 98%. They asked me if I was able to breathe comfortably without oxygen to which I replied in the affirmative. They decided to take me off the oxygen also, completely. The lead doctor turned to Trish and said, "your husband is a good man". Being a muslim, this was probably all he could say about all these miraculous interventions, which were beyond their understanding and for which they had no explanation.

I knew God had taken over when He kicked the chest tube out and I had been expectant of His clear intervention all along. He, indeed, sent forth His Word and healed me – the very Word which we had held on to right from the start, in the face of contrary evidence. *Hallelujah*!

I was still having sporadic bouts of coughing but I decided not to be distracted by any symptoms. I was going to remain steadfast in continuously declaring the truth of His Word until it manifested in my body.

Meanwhile, I was still testing positive for TB bacteria. They had to take three sputum samples at a time for testing and I found it so difficult to cough up these specimens that they had to induce it! Yet, they maintained their diagnosis of end-stage TB. The funny thing was that each time they tested, the outcome was negative for the first two but positive for the last one, consistently! They were completely clueless as to why the specimens were collected under very random circumstances and yet the results followed a consistent pattern for quite a significant period of time. *Whoa*! Quite uncanny that!

One weekend afternoon, the doctor on duty asked me if I was still coughing blood, much to my wildest amazement. This was an external doctor who came to relieve the house physician over weekends. Obviously, someone had made up this story and again added it to my medical records. I stated emphatically that I had never coughed up blood. The doctor did not react to my remonstrations and continued her perfunctory examination to ascertain my condition.

It dawned on me that there were simply no answers to all the questions that were coming up from either side. One thing I knew for sure though was that God was going to finish what He had begun. I wasn't interested in their planned course of actions any longer. My prayer was that my stay in that hospital would bring glory to Him. I could perceive that the medical staff knew at this point that a Power greater than their knowledge was at work in my body, albeit they would not admit it.

FREEDOM AT LAST

Yipeeeee!!! Yayyy!!! Praise God!!! On that memorable day, the news I had been awaiting for so long hit me in waves. It was the duty nurse who first dropped a hint when she started her shift that the latest results from the lab were indicating negative for all three tests! Then, the next morning the team of doctors invaded my room to officially communicate the news to me. I was beside myself with excitement! I was now out of isolation so I could now wander away from my room for the first time in more than six months. I had been in a de-facto prison cell. It was exhilarating to be free once again – to walk unaided within the premises.

Suddenly, some of the staff who had been carrying out their duties in my room in a detached and mechanical manner began putting in a great deal of effort to be nice. It is sad and rather unfortunate how some people relate with you based on your prevailing circumstances. There was a particular male nurse who flashed his teeth at me for the first time only when the news eventually got to him.

"Ah Mr. Charles!" he exclaimed. "I hear your test results came out negative; that is very good."

I acknowledged curtly, as he waxed unusually chatty. Human beings...hmmm.

I recalled my prayer that God would be glorified in that hospital. Even if they didn't verbalise it, my prayer was that they would perceive the power of God behind all the events which simply defied medical explanation that had unfolded before their very eyes. God is indeed faithful and true! The medical fraternity in that hospital had been truly and thoroughly confounded – a prayer one of our friends, Brendan had raised. Praise God!

One afternoon I got a surprise visit from my friend Grant, the same one who somehow broke through protocol and security and made an almost angelic appearance in my room when I was in intensive care. Wow! This time around Trish was with me and he was happy to find me in a much better state than before. He shared with us how the church had been lifting us up in prayer and admitted that he was really afraid for me when he saw he saw my emaciated body on the earlier visit. We all thanked God for His faithfulness and he prayed with us before leaving. Such sincere demonstration of love! Our friend, Pastor Zeal, also spent time in my room on several occasions, praying with us and encouraging us. God had our backs all along.

For the first time in some six months, I could wander away from my room on my own. I was still underweight and rather frail but after literally learning how to walk again in my room, I could move about unaided. As I went on my daily walk in the corridors and especially up and down the flight of steps, I mused on how fragile we all are. Here was I, a fitness buff, now trying to recover my muscle strength all over again. Nevertheless, I had set my face like flint and really looked forward to these daily walks accompanied by Trish most of the time. My body had taken a real battering over these six-months from the debilitating effects of sickness and all the medication that I had to take.

On one of these walks, with Trish by my side, I thought I saw the lead doctor who had admitted me in the distance. I hadn't seen him for nearly two months because he had been on leave. As we closed in on him, I noticed that he was tossing his head from side to side, and then straining forward, he raised his hand to a level just above his eyes. I could tell that he was struggling with trying to confirm my identity. Obviously, he hadn't expected to return from his leave to find me not only alive, but walking unaided around the hospital.

When he came close enough to recognise me clearly, he surged forward. I stretched out my hand to shake his, but he ignored it completely and rather gave me a big, warm bear hug. He was very thrilled to see me out of isolation and walking about – resembling nothing of the grim picture that he had painted with his original prognosis. He looked me square in the face and said with careful emphasis, "you are a great man; you must write a book!"

He left me with those words, excused himself and went on his way. I knew that being a muslim, he was actually acknowledging God's hand in my situation without making a direct reference to that reality. I had prayed that God would be glorified through my stay in the hospital and this was the closest verbal acknowledgement. I remember my friend Brendan Law, who had said that the medical community would be confounded when I walked out of that hospital. The lead doctor's remarks confirmed that. They really didn't have any medical explanation for my recovery from a 'grave' situation! Indeed, only God has the final say!

CHECKOUT TIME

It was time for me to leave the hospital – the same place where, ironically, we had come to pray for the sick on a few occasions prior to my confinement. My weight was checked after I had come out of isolation and after bottoming out at 53 kilograms for more than three months, I had begun to regain my weight. By now, I could take a shower without getting breathless in the process. I chose to use the staircase instead of the elevator during my daily exercise and I noticed I was not running short of breath like before. I was very grateful to God for healing me and I was elated by all the positive changes I was experiencing. I could perceive that my sojourn in that place was practically over.

The devil, however, was still roaring about like a lion, trying hard to put fear in me through the doctors' decisions and remarks. First of all, the issue of surgery came up again as they claimed there were bullae (some kind of air pockets) in my lungs that could only be removed surgically. I had to wait for about a week while they conferred with a cardiothoracic surgeon in the hospital, where I was initially supposed to have been transferred to. I kept on confessing the Word and declaring that I was already healed and that the manifestation was just a matter of time.

In the meanwhile, I had to do what they call a 'high altitude simulation test' to ascertain if my oxygen saturation would be adequate during air travel without recourse to medical oxygen. Consequently, a hood was placed over my head; I was isolated from the room atmosphere and air with reduced oxygen content introduced for about twenty minutes, while the key parameters were monitored. My breathing was pretty normal and the positive results reflected that.

The medical team came to inform me that, following close scrutiny of my latest CT scans and X-ray images over the course of a few days, the cardiothoracic surgeon had finally given his opinion on the issue of surgery. Bottom line was that surgery was not required!

Hallelujah!! I remember praying and asking God to perform the surgery Himself when the subject first came up. I declared, "You are my great Physician; You made this body and only You can fix it perfectly!!" I had seen facts change during my stay at the hospital but the truth of God's Word remained unchanging! This reality only consolidated my faith and trust in His Word, regardless of whatever medical evidence was presented before me. *"...let God be true but every man a liar"* (Romans 3:4).

There was still a battle raging though because the very next day the lead doctor was back in my room with quite a grim face. After greeting me, he made his way to the only window in the room, overlooking the car park, then turned round with his arms behind him.

"There are some decisions that the patient has to take in a situation where the odds that something could go wrong are 50 – 50", he began. He informed me that in the low pressure environment of an airplane in flight, there was a fifty per cent chance that the bullae or trapped air pockets that they had seen in my lungs could rupture and trigger severe respiratory distress. This could prove fatal according to him!

He then asked me if I could travel to Ghana by road! I stared at him in disbelief for a moment and decided to excuse his rather pathetic ignorance of the geographical location of Ghana. I told him that travel by road was certainly not an option. Then, he suggested that I look into the possibility of travelling by ship and left me to think about it! I was not fazed at all at this stage. What had unfolded in the hospital right before my eyes made me believe absolutely in the reality of my healing. Any fear that the news was intended to invoke was immediately diffused.

The next day he was back in my room to inform me that, following a full board meeting of consultants on my case, a final decision had been reached to the effect that I could not travel by air. Again, I was advised to travel by land or by sea!! He asked me if I had made any travel arrangements to which question I replied in the negative. I had planned to do that once I had been discharged.

I requested a medical report covering the period of hospitalization and was asked to see the accountant to close my account, as it were. When Trish asked for the bill, the accountant indicated to our amazement that we had nothing to pay! We asked him to check carefully but he maintained that there was nothing to pay. He asked Trish to sign a release form and gave her a prescription to collect the rest of my medication from the pharmacy.

Now, this was another miracle! There had definitely been a bill: on two occasions they had asked me how I was going to pay because it was mounting and I didn't have acceptable insurance. So what happened? We just thanked God for this miracle. When we shared this story with a friend who happened to be working as an accountant in another hospital at the time, she blurted out, "my brother, this is a miracle!" She indicated that the bill covering in-patient care for a non-citizen for that period of time could easily hit around one hundred and fifty thousand U.S. dollars!

When they first asked me how I was going to pay my bill, I remember asking them to just let me have the bill when it was ready. I had cast this care on Him because He cares for me (1 Peter 5:7) and I had reminded God that He had promised to supply all my needs according to His riches in glory by Christ Jesus (Philippians 4:19). Besides this, we had a Malaysian friend, who also insisted that we call her to come and pick up any bill given to me because her boss, who was a philanthropist, had offered to pay all my medical expenses! This was indeed overwhelming for us!

We had seen God's hand upon us throughout this entire episode at the hospital - His healing power, His provision and help from His children, whom He had strategically placed among the medical staff. Surely, there must have been a divine purpose for my sojourn in that hospital for nearly six-and-a-half months. I pray that God will reveal this fully to me in due course. I counted myself blessed to experience the power of God in a way that had considerably strengthened my faith in His Word. I was leaving the hospital with a much different perspective on sicknesses and diseases.

In the words of the song *Through It All* by Andrae Crouch,

Through it all
Through it all
I've learned to trust in Jesus
I've learned to trust in God

Through it all
Through it all
I've learned to depend upon His Word

These words encapsulated my experience during this season, for which I am truly thankful and grateful. I now have a deeper appreciation and assurance of His love for me.

On September 28, 2014, exactly one hundred and ninety-two days after being admitted, I walked out of the premier hospital in Abu Dhabi and headed home with Trish. *Phew!* As we drove along the broad streets of the city centre, I mused over all that had transpired in the last six months or so. This had been one raging storm but Jesus had been with me throughout, and as I engaged the Word I saw His mighty deliverance.

I was still underweight, and I had to stay put for some time before easing myself gently into everyday life once again. We agreed that I was healed completely because of the finished work of Christ Jesus, just as we had maintained right from the onset.

Our dear friend Charles Ahene, a compatriot and an anaesthesiologist at the hospital, had been very concerned since he heard that I could not travel by air. He called soon after I had been discharged to find out about my travel plans in the light of the doctors' final opinion.

I assured him that we fully appreciated their concerns and that we had also prayed about it. We had complete peace about proceeding with booking flights for the trip back home. Having begun in the Spirit, we were not going to continue in the flesh at this stage.

> *"Are you so foolish? Having begun by the Spirit, are you now being perfected by the flesh?"* – Galatians 3:3

He pondered for a moment and expressed his belief that the same God who had brought me thus far will be with me during the flight.

IT'S NOT ABOUT ME,
NO, NOT AT ALL!

A couple of weeks after being discharged, I felt strong enough to go to church. I had really missed fellowship for a long time – about seven months, altogether – and was eagerly looking forward to seeing all our friends once again. A lot of them had been faithfully supporting us in prayer, financially and even cooking for the boys to relieve the pressure on Trish a bit.

As we entered the hall where we held our meetings, I realised there were a lot of new faces. There must have been about two hundred people in the room that morning. Word had gone out that I was out of hospital but my appearance that morning was meant to be a surprise. We picked out a lot of faces beaming with excitement in the congregation, some of them waving wildly at us, as we took our seats right in front.

After the announcements were read and just before the sermon commenced, I made my way briskly to the front of the auditorium. I went to greet and hug the pastor Matt and his wife Rana, whom I had obviously not seen for as long as I had been away. Then, I turned around to thank the entire congregation for their prayers and to give glory to God for healing me. I shared the story of God's mighty intervention during my sojourn at the hospital. Everyone had eventually come to know, at a point, that I had been diagnosed with end-stage tuberculosis. What most people didn't know, though, which I disclosed to them, was how the doctor who admitted me gave a very grim prognosis at the onset, suggesting to Trish to inform the Ghana Embassy in Dubai to prepare to transport a corpse back home, referring to me.

I testified that because of the mighty hand of God upon me, that same doctor upon his return from a long leave, came to give me a big hug when our paths crossed during one of my daily walks. I told them how he had said to me, "you are a great man; you must write a book!" I shared that for a muslim, short of a direct reference to a miracle from God, that amounted to a tacit admission that they were truly and thoroughly confounded.

Just when I started sharing all this, the most amazing scene unfolded before my eyes. The entire congregation started rising to their feet, one after the other, and within a moment there was a standing ovation, which lasted for a couple of minutes. Wow! Glory be to God! Hallelujah!

In that moment, it dawned on me yet again that this whole trial was not about me at all. It was all about Him! The devil had made a beeline for my faith but by the grace of God I had held on and emerged victorious. I went on to encourage the congregation that if God had brought me out of my sickbed, indeed my deathbed, and presented me healed and well before their eyes, then there was surely no situation they were going through that God could not deal with. I thanked them, once again, and took my seat to allow the service to continue.

After the service, a lot of our friends came over to embrace us and thank God with us. A few new worshippers also came around and shared with us how my testimony had impacted them. They all confessed that their faith had been greatly kindled just by hearing my story, some with tears rolling down their cheeks. What made it even more poignant, according to them, was the fact that they were actually beholding the bearer of this testimony in real time. Hearing a live testimony from the lips of the narrator is usually more palpable than reading one from an unknown and unseen beneficiary of God's grace, any time.

The more I pondered this, the deeper it resonated within my entire being that it wasn't about me at all. It was so that the Lord may be exalted. I perceived that the faith of many had already been impacted positively by my story, and there was no telling how far this impact would reach. Some sought my permission to share the testimony with their families in their native countries, which I heartily granted. Truly, I felt privileged that God would use my story to impact so many lives. I did not understand how this was working out exactly but I knew that more pieces would fall into place later on. His ways are not our ways and are indeed past finding out. Glory be to God in the highest!!

EPILOGUE

We began winding up our affairs in Abu Dhabi and saying our adieux to our friends and brethren of 'like precious faith'. During this time, we had a lot of invitations for coffee or a meal, which we seized as opportunities to share my testimony in more detail than we had done publicly. As we kept sharing it was evident both to our hearers and also to ourselves that God was on to something really big to His own glory. We could only imagine how many lives were being affected as the story spread.

Clearly, a real-time testimony of God stepping into a 'dead' situation by reason of exercising faith in His Word had a greater effect on the faith of believers when there was some acquaintance with the testifier. Knowledge of His Word is not enough. We need to put that knowledge to work by acting on it. The Word says that we can speak to mountains that loom in our horizon to be removed and be cast into the sea and we shall have what we say if we don't doubt. In the book of James, trials are referred to as the testing of faith, and until our faith is tested, our knowledge of the Word remains theoretical. It is only within this context that one can count it all joy when one goes through trials.

I share the story of a Christian minister, who was travelling by air and found himself seated next to a racing car test driver. After exchanging the usual pleasantries, the minister asked the test driver to tell him a bit more about his apparently interesting work. The latter proceeded to explain that after the racing car had been designed and performance specifications determined, it was his job to drive the car under various pre-determined conditions to verify the accuracy of the performance data. Then, and only then, could the engine performance specifications be presented to potential buyers. In other words, they must be in a position to guarantee the stated performance specifications within agreed conditions. Phew!

I find in this story an excellent analogy to the trials and tribulations that come our way as believers. Jesus said that in this world we would have tribulation, but He also said that we should take heart because He has overcome the world. To live as overcomers, we must believe in Him and place our faith in His finished work.

Now that's where the rubber meets the road; putting your money where your mouth is, as they say. When you receive the revelation that the facts are not the same as the truth, and also that the former can change, then you begin to speak His Word over every situation that is contrary to your glorious destiny. You also begin to take faith-based action based on the revealed truth especially, when it goes against logic or reason.

That is tough: it's always a fight and our faith is the actual target of the devil's attacks. "Fight the good fight of faith and lay hold on eternal life..." – 1 Timothy 6:12. Faith doesn't make sense and yet that is how God has determined that the children of the Kingdom should live.

"Now the just shall live by faith; but if anyone draws back, My soul has no pleasure in him"
—Hebrews 10:38

We can only achieve this victory that overcomes the world, even our faith, when we put the Word to work. Our glorious inheritance in Christ remains like the stated performance data of that racing car. We can only tap into it by engaging the Word in much the same way that the test driver can only experience the capacity of the car by actually driving it.

"Thus also faith by itself, if it does not have works, is dead"—James 2:17

Believing is simply not enough; we must act on what we believe.

"You believe that there is one God. You do well. Even the demons believe — and tremble!"
—James 2:19

As we take those steps of faith, tottering perhaps, at the beginning, but firmer and bolder as we move from victory to victory, our faith becomes stronger just like a muscle does when it is exercised. The key issue of our identity in Christ comes into focus as we realize that we need to be secure in that in order to access our inheritance as redeemed children of God through faith.

God's Word is true, forever settled in Heaven and He watches eagerly over it to perform it. Our professed belief is only validated when our actions are consistent with it. Otherwise, our belief in God's Word is simply equivalent to mental assent and we will be unable to appropriate the glorious inheritance that the finished work of Christ has procured for us.

> *"Then said the Lord to me, You have seen well, for I am alert and active, watching over My word to perform it"* – Jeremiah 1:12

For both Trish and I, this has been a journey of faith. Trish's perspective on illness and disease, and the limitations of medical science was positively impacted as she closely observed all that unfolded from her 'ring-side' position. As far as my case was concerned, she simply set aside her medical knowledge and stood on the truth of God's Word as we both affirmed and claimed my healing as a finished work. God had moved in response to our faith, as He always does, and we cannot but give Him alone all the glory and all the praise. I now consult Him as my Great Physician and Healer before I talk to anyone else.

Out of Abu Dhabi we flew, two months after I was discharged from hospital, leaving the golden sands, ranges of dunes, wonderful friends and memorable events behind us. A season in our lives had just come to a close. It was a long flight to Accra - almost nine hours – and though I didn't give it a thought, nothing ruptured in my lungs, neither did I experience any respiratory distress. The devil is, indeed, a liar and the father of liars! Thank God we had chosen to believe God's report over the devil's, presented under the guise of medical prognosis or opinion.

As we touched down in Accra, we just thanked God for bringing us safely home and for His faithfulness through it all. Our faith had truly been tested and God had shown Himself faithful as we took His Word at face value, and made our boast in Him. We had practically experienced the truth of His Word and learnt that, indeed, living by faith is not an option - it is essential, a sine qua non, the only means by which a child of God may live.

"For whatever is born of God overcomes the world; and this is the victory that has overcome the world – our faith" – 1 John 5: 4

In conclusion, it is my heartfelt desire that as many as read this testimony or hear it from the lips of another will be encouraged to take God at His Word. I believe that somehow it is received better when the narrator is known to, or acquainted with, the hearer. However, God has His own way of using a testimony in ways we never are able to imagine or fully comprehend, in order to accomplish His will and purpose on Earth.

"And they overcame Him because of the blood of the Lamb and because of the word of their testimony..." – Revelation 12:11a

Faith is not logical, neither does it make sense. Faith is engaging the infallible Word of Him Who is not a man that He should lie. That's how the awesome power of God is released in our lives to bring us to our glorious destiny. It is that switch that we've got to flip to allow power to come through to provide light to chase away darkness.

The good news for those who are not sure if they have any faith at all is that God has given to every man the measure of faith. This faith can grow when it is exercised, just like a muscle in the human body.

> *"...as God has dealt to each one a measure of faith"* – Romans 12:3b

Jesus came into the world to save it:

> *"For God did not send His Son into the world to condemn the world, but that the world through Him might be saved"* – John 3:17

The word 'saved' is derived from the Greek, *'sozo'* and not only means spiritual rebirth, but also includes healing, preservation, restoration, deliverance(from destruction), protection, prosperity and wholeness. This is the salvation package available to every believer and we can only appropriate it by exercising our faith.

My prayer is that as your faith is stirred up by this testimony you will be motivated to dig into the Word to know what is already yours in Christ and to possess it practically. Amen!

HEALING SCRIPTURES

I wish to share our favourite healing scriptures which we believed in, held on to tenaciously, and affirmed audibly over my body until my change manifested. The Bible says that the Word is life to those that find it and health to all their flesh (Proverbs 4:22)! I pray that you will have a tangible experience of God's power as you believe and speak His Word over your life. Amen!

"...If you diligently heed the voice of the Lord your God and do what is right in his sight, give ear to His commandments and keep all His statutes, I will put none of the diseases on you which I have brought on the Egyptians. For I am the lord who heals you."– Exodus 15:26

"And in the thirty-ninth year of his reign, Asa became diseased in his feet, and his malady was severe; yet in his disease he did not seek the Lord, but the physicians." – 2 Chronicles 16:12

"Bless the Lord, O my soul, and forget not all His benefits: Who forgives all your iniquities, who heals all your diseases…" – Psalms 103:2-3

"He sent His Word and healed them and delivered them from their destructions." Psalms 107:20

"My son, give attention to my words; incline your ear to my sayings. Do not let them depart from your eyes; keep them in the midst of your heart; for they are life to those who find them, and health to all their flesh." – Proverbs 4: 20-22

"But He was wounded for our transgressions, He was bruised for our iniquities; the chastisement for our peace was upon Him, and by His stripes we are healed." – Isaiah 53:5

"For I will restore health to you and heal you of your wounds," says the Lord, "because they have called you an outcast saying: "this is Zion; no one seeks her." – Jeremiah 30:17

"This was to fulfil what was spoken through Isaiah the prophet: "He Himself took our infirmities and bore our sicknesses." – Matthew 8:17

"How God anointed Jesus of Nazareth with the Holy Spirit and with power who went about doing good and healing all who were oppressed by the devil, for God was with Him." – Acts 10:38

"Jesus Christ is the same yesterday, today, and forever." – Hebrews 13:8

"Who Himself bore our sins in His own body on the tree, that we, having died to sins, might live for righteousness – by whose stripes you were healed." – 1 Peter 2:24

"Beloved, I pray that you may prosper in all things and be in health, just as your soul prospers." – 3 John 2

ABOUT THE AUTHOR

Charles Richardson was born, and grew up in Accra, Ghana. He is a mechanical engineer by profession and has spent most of his working life in the aviation industry as a licensed aircraft engineer. He has had a varied working experience having worked with a diversity of airlines based both in Ghana and abroad.

He is a member of the Catch the Anointing Centre headquarters denomination of the UDOLGC (United Denominations Originating from the Lighthouse Group of Churches). He lives in Tema, Ghana with his wife Patricia and their two sons, Jude and Joshua.